ABE LINCOLN
LOVED ANIMALS

Written by
**ELLEN
JACKSON**

Illustrated by
**DORIS
ETTLINGER**

Fido, the Lincolns' dog, about 1860.

ALBERT WHITMAN & COMPANY, MORTON GROVE, ILLINOIS

Long ago, in the wooded hollows of Kentucky, lived a young boy who loved animals.

In the spring, the boy, Abraham Lincoln, discovered a mother fox with her babies. In the autumn, he watched raccoons gather acorns in the woods.

From an early age, Abraham saw that animals felt pain and pleasure and had lives of their own.

The boy's family lived on a farm, first in Kentucky and later in Indiana. Abraham and his sister, Sarah, fetched water, chopped firewood, and helped their mother plant seeds and grind corn. Abraham's papa often hunted rabbits or deer. Hunting was a way of life for those who lived on the frontier. Everyone worked hard to put food on the table.

When Abraham grew older, his family expected him to help feed the family. One day, he spotted a flock of wild turkeys. He took aim with a rifle and shot one of the birds. But the sight of the dying turkey filled him with sorrow. I will never hunt large animals again, he thought to himself. And he didn't.

Other children would sometimes hurt animals, but not Abraham. Once at school, Abraham saw his friends putting red-hot coals on the back of a turtle. He had to speak up and stop them.

"Cruelty to animals is wrong," he told the children. "Even an ant values its life."

When he had grown into a young man, Abraham moved to Springfield, Illinois, and worked as a lawyer. When he was only twenty, he made a speech that so impressed everyone it was printed in the newspaper. Important people began to notice him. But Abraham still took time to help animals.

One day, he and his friends were riding in the country. As Abraham passed a grove of wild plum and crab apple trees, he stopped. Two baby birds had been blown like leaves from their nest.

He dismounted, gathered up the birds, shinnied up the tree, and put them back.

"What foolishness!" said Abraham's friend Joshua Speed. "Now you've gone and ruined your good suit."

"I could not have slept well tonight if I had not saved those birds," said Abraham quietly. He didn't care if his friends laughed at him.

At a dance in 1839, Abraham met a friendly, spunky girl named Mary Todd. Three years later, they were married. During the next eleven years, the couple had four boys: Robert, Eddie, Willie, and Tad.

Abraham found room in his house for cats, kittens, and dogs. He and the boys liked to walk in the woods, looking for insects, butterflies, and rocks.

Abraham traveled to nearby towns to work with people who needed a lawyer. He rode Old Bob, who was probably his favorite animal companion. After a ride, Abraham would examine Bob's feet, give him a carrot, and rub his nose.

A floppy-eared dog named Fido came to live with the Lincoln family. Abraham and Fido would often walk down the street with the dog carrying a parcel in his mouth. When Abraham stopped for a haircut at Billy's Barber Shop, Fido waited patiently outside—unless a group of children came by. Then Fido jumped and played until Abraham was ready to go home.

Abraham served a term in the United States House of Representatives. In 1860, he became a candidate for president of the United States. When he won the election, the Lincoln family prepared to move to the White House in Washington, D.C.

Sadly, Abraham decided that Fido would not accompany the family. The train trip would be long and difficult, and the Lincoln family had a large amount of baggage to carry.

Abraham asked a neighboring family, the Rolls, to take Fido. He gave them the horsehair sofa that was the dog's favorite piece of furniture.

"You must promise me," said Abraham to the Roll boys, "not to scold Fido for entering the house with muddy paws. He should never be tied up alone in the backyard, and whenever he scratches at the door, he must be let in."

Fido's new family agreed to everything. How could they say no to the new president? Before the Lincoln family left for Washington, they had a picture taken of Fido so they would never forget him. Photography was still new, and this was the first picture ever taken of a presidential pet.

In Washington, the Lincoln family filled their new home with pets—rabbits, dogs, cats, and even a couple of goats. Tad, Abraham's youngest son, once hitched the goats to a chair and drove them through the White House, scattering a group of women attending a reception.

A guest noticed how the president pampered the family cat, who sat next to him during dinner. "Don't you think it is shameful for Mr. Lincoln to feed Tabby with a gold fork?" Mrs. Lincoln asked the guest.

"If the gold fork was good enough for President Buchanan, I think it is good enough for Tabby," said Abraham Lincoln.

The new president had many problems. In 1860, the United States consisted of some states that permitted slavery and others that didn't. Slavery was a terrible evil that allowed white people to own black people. Slaves were made to work hard and were often treated cruelly. Abraham Lincoln had promised to ban slavery in the territories that might someday become states. "I believe this Government cannot endure permanently half slave and half free," he had said.

When Abraham Lincoln was elected, many of the southern, slave-holding states seceded, or left, the Union to form their own government. But Abraham Lincoln was willing to fight to keep the country together.

Soon the United States was plunged into a terrible civil war. Abraham Lincoln realized that slavery must end if the Union was to be saved. In 1863, he issued the Emancipation Proclamation, freeing all the slaves in the rebel states. Some people hated the president for this act. Others thought he was a great man. Abraham Lincoln had courageously committed the United States government to the cause of freedom.

The war continued. On the battlefield, the dead were heaped as high as "autumn leaves." Abraham's face was haggard and gray with constant worry.

The president found comfort in the company of animals. On a visit to the headquarters of General Grant, leader of the Union army, he came upon three tiny kittens whose mother had recently died. He picked them up, stroked them, and said to the colonel in charge, "I hope you will see that these poor little motherless waifs are given plenty of milk and treated kindly." The colonel promised the kittens would be well treated.

Despite the war, Abraham was never too busy for his boys. One year, just before Christmas, Tad found a huge turkey wandering on the White House grounds. Tad named him Jack, looped a piece of string around his neck, and led him around to meet the White House staff.

"I see you've met your Christmas dinner," said the cook.

What! Was Jack to be killed and served for Christmas? Tad ran to the president's office where his father was in an important meeting.

"Papa!" said Tad. "Please don't let them kill Jack. He's a good turkey and doesn't deserve to die!"

Abraham listened quietly. Long ago, he had shot a turkey. Perhaps the regret he had felt then welled up in his heart again. But this time things would end differently.

"He *is* a good turkey, Tad," said Abraham. "And I'll pardon him. After all, I am the president."

Then Abraham Lincoln wrote out a presidential pardon for Jack, changing him from a meal into a member of the family.

In 1864, President Lincoln was elected to serve another four-year term. But in April 1865, a few days after the Civil War had ended and the nation was reunited, Abraham Lincoln was shot and killed by an assassin. People all over the country mourned the death of their beloved leader.

When President Lincoln was buried in Springfield, Illinois, Old Bob, wearing a blanket with silver fringe, walked behind the funeral procession. Fido, too, was brought back to his old home to greet the mourners.

Today, people everywhere honor Abraham Lincoln, the president who saved the Union and issued the Emancipation Proclamation.

Abraham's love for animals lives on. Each Thanksgiving, the president of the United States "pardons" a turkey—just as Abraham Lincoln did more than one hundred years ago.

Abraham Lincoln's kind heart had room for all creatures, great and small. A Native American legend says that when humans die, they are greeted by all the animals they befriended when they were alive. If so, voices from the air, the water, and the land must have welcomed Abraham Lincoln home.

Few people in the nineteenth century worried about the welfare of animals. Wild animals provided food for families who struggled daily to stay alive. Even pets and domestic animals were treated in ways that would be considered cruel today.

Abraham Lincoln was unusually kind to animals. He did not like to hunt, though he lived at a time and in a place where men with guns often shot animals and birds. From early childhood, he believed that animals, as well as people, should be treated fairly and with compassion. His stepsister, Matilda Johnston, said that Abraham even defended the right of ants to live in peace.

Many stories about Abraham Lincoln's love for animals were told after his death by friends and family. For this reason, historians can't always know if a particular story has been exaggerated. In this book, I've chosen those stories that are most likely to be authentic.

For a campaign biography that John L. Scripps prepared in 1860, Lincoln wrote about the turkey he shot. Nathaniel Grigsby, one of Abraham Lincoln's schoolmates, and Matilda Johnston are the original sources for the turtle and ant stories. These stories are retold in *The Every-Day Life of Abraham Lincoln* by Francis Fisher Browne and in an essay in the *Journal of the Illinois State Historical Society 93, no. 3* (1999). Joshua Speed was a friend of Lincoln's who observed him restoring the birds to their nest. The incident was recorded in the now rare *Lincoln Memorial Album of Immortelles*, published in 1890, and it has subsequently been reported by many others, such as Douglas L. Wilson in *Honor's Voice*. The account of Lincoln feeding Tabby was told by the Reverend Noyes Miner to his daughter. It appears in several sources including *Rare Personal Accounts of Abraham Lincoln*, edited by William R. Feeheley and Bill Snack. The story of Tad and the turkey is recorded by Louis A. Warren in his book *Lincoln's Youth: Indiana Years, Seven to Twenty-One, 1816-1830.*

Stories of Abraham Lincoln's other pets are recorded in many sources, including *White House Pets* by Margaret Truman, *Lincoln's Animal Friends* by Ruth Painter Randall, and *Honor's Voice* by Douglas L. Wilson. In *Abe Lincoln Loved Animals*, some of Lincoln's remarks were quoted verbatim; others were paraphrased from accounts given by those who knew him.

BIBLIOGRAPHY

Beatty, Albert R. "Dogs Ever Were a Joy to Lincoln." *American Kennel Gazette* 50 (February 1, 1933): 9-13 and 77-80.

Browne, Francis Fisher. *The Every-Day Life of Abraham Lincoln*. Lincoln: University of Nebraska Press, 1995.

Burlingame, Michael. *The Inner World of Abraham Lincoln*. Urbana: University of Illinois Press, 1994.

Donald, David Herbert. *Lincoln*. New York: Simon and Schuster, 1996.

Feeheley, William R., and Bill Snack, eds. *Rare Personal Accounts of Abraham Lincoln*. Cadillac, Mich.: Railsplitter Publishing, 2005.

Havlik, Robert J. "Abraham Lincoln and the Reverend Dr. James Smith: Lincoln's Presbyterian Experience in Springfield." *Journal of the Illinois State Historical Society* 93, no. 3 (1999): 222-37.

Holzer, Harold. *Lincoln As I Knew Him: Gossip, Tributes, and Revelations from His Best Friends and Worst Enemies*. Chapel Hill, N. C.: Algonquin Books of Chapel Hill, 1999.

Hunt, Eugenia Jones. "My Personal Recollections of Abraham and Mary Todd Lincoln." *Abraham Lincoln Quarterly* 3 (March 1945): 251.

Keneally, Thomas. *Abraham Lincoln*. New York: Viking Press, 2003.

Lincoln, Abraham. "Autobiography Written for John L. Scripps," *circa* June 1860, in Roy P. Basler, ed., *The Collected Works of Abraham Lincoln*, 9 vols. New Brunswick: Rutgers University Press, 1953-1955, vol. 4: 60-68.

Miller, William Lee. *Lincoln's Virtues: An Ethical Biography*. New York: Alfred A. Knopf, 2002.

Oates, Stephen B. *With Malice Toward None: The Life of Abraham Lincoln*. New York: Harper & Row, 1977.

Ostendorf, Lloyd. *Abraham Lincoln: The Boy, the Man*. Springfield, Ill.: P. H. Wagner, 1962.

Randall, Ruth Painter. *Lincoln's Animal Friends: Incidents about Abraham Lincoln and Animals, Woven into an Intimate Story of His Life*. Boston: Little, Brown, 1958.

_____. *Lincoln's Sons*. Boston: Little, Brown, 1955.

Rowan, Ray, and Janis Brooke. *First Dogs: American Presidents and Their Best Friends*. Chapel Hill, N. C.: Algonquin Books of Chapel Hill, 1997.

Sandburg, Carl. *Abraham Lincoln: The Prairie Years and the War Years*. New York: Galahad Books, 1993.

Truman, Margaret. *White House Pets*. New York: David McKay, 1969.

Warren, Louis A. *Lincoln's Youth: Indiana Years, Seven to Twenty-One, 1816-1830*. Indianapolis: Indiana Historical Society; Reprint edition, 2002.

Wilson, Douglas L. *Honor's Voice: The Transformation of Abraham Lincoln*. New York: Alfred A. Knopf, 1998.

To Robin, Smoky, Daphne, Bailey, Duffy, Stanley, Dolly Ruth, Bo, and special animals everywhere.

A number of Lincoln scholars read, commented, and suggested changes to the text of this manuscript.
These include Michael Bishop, Mike Capps, Roger Norton, Timothy P. Townsend, William D. Pederson, and
Frank J. Williams. Thanks to you all for your generosity and invaluable assistance.
Thanks also to my editor, Abby Levine, for her insistence on a high standard of excellence.—E.J.

Ellen Jackson is the author of more than sixty books for children, including
the award-winning *Turn of the Century* and *Earth Mother*.

To Rosemary Kent—D.E.

Doris Ettlinger has also illustrated *Pilgrim Cat* and *Morris and Buddy: The Story of the First Seeing Eye Dog*.

Library of Congress Cataloging-in-Publication Data

Jackson, Ellen B., 1943-
Abe Lincoln loved animals / by Ellen Jackson ; illustrated by Doris Ettlinger.
p. cm.
ISBN 978-0-8075-0123-8
1. Lincoln, Abraham, 1809-1865—Anecdotes—Juvenile literature. 2. Presidents—United States—Pets—Anecdotes—Juvenile literature.
3. Presidents—United States—Biography—Anecdotes—Juvenile literature. 4. Pets—United States—Anecdotes—Juvenile literature.
5. Human-animal relationships—United States—Anecdotes—Juvenile literature. I. Ettlinger, Doris, ill. II. Title.
E457.905.J325 2008 973.7092—dc22 2007052610

Text copyright © 2008 by Ellen Jackson. Illustrations copyright © 2008 by Doris Ettlinger.
Published in 2008 by Albert Whitman & Company, 6340 Oakton Street, Morton Grove, Illinois 60053-2723.
Published simultaneously in Canada by Fitzhenry & Whiteside, Markham, Ontario. All rights reserved. No part of this book may be reproduced or transmitted in any form or
by any means, electronic or mechanical, including photocopying, recording, or by any information storage and retrieval system, without permission in writing from the publisher.
Printed in China through B & P International Ltd.
10 9 8 7 6 5 4 3 2 1

The design is by Carol Gildar.

For more information about Albert Whitman & Company, please visit our web site at www.albertwhitman.com.

The photo of Fido on p. 1 is Courtesy of the Abraham Lincoln Presidential Library.